Caring, Sharing & Getting Along

50 Perfect Poems for Promoting Good Behavior in Your Classroom

by Betsy Franco

S C H O L A S T I C
PROFESSIONAL BOOKS

New York • Toronto • London • Auckland • Sydney • Mexico City • New Delhi • Hong Kong

For my good friend Lorraine

Special thanks to Talley Kenyon and Debbie Maine for sharing their wisdom with me. Debbie Maine, a wonderful Highland School teacher, created and shared the "Giving Encouragement/Using Put-Ups" activity with me.

I couldn't have written this book without the help of Katy Obringer and Maya Spector, librarians at the Palo Alto Children's Library.

Acknowledgments

"At the School Fair" and "Manners on the Monkey Bars" are from *Poem of the Week Book 2* by Betsy Franco. Teaching Resource Center, 1999.

"What Goes Around" is from *Poem of the Week Book 3* by Betsy Franco. Teaching Resource Center, 1999.

"Making New Friends" is variation of a poem from *All About Me!* by Betsy Franco and Friends. Scholastic, 2000.

"How People Feel About Me," "I'm Special, You're Special," and "Feelings" are from *All About Me!* by Betsy Franco and Friends. Scholastic, 2000.

"Rules at School" is a variation of a poem published in *More Phonics Through Poetry* by Babs Bell Hajdusiewicz. Good Year Books, 1997.

Cover design by Judy Kamilar

Cover illustration by Dawn Apperly

Interior design by Ellen Matlach Hassell for Boultinghouse & Boultinghouse, Inc.

Interior illustration by Anthony Lewis

ISBN: 0-439-20105-5

Copyright © 2000 by Betsy Franco.

Contents

The Best Me I Can Be

Manners and Rules

Getting Along

Introduction

Every teacher wants to build a feeling of community in his or her classroom—a caring, sharing community where children feel respected and appreciated. To start building such an environment, you often must do some basic teaching about values and manners and reinforce that teaching throughout the school year. The classroom offers abundant opportunities for giving children the tools for solving conflicts and getting along together.

What better way to introduce and reinforce these valuable lessons than through poetry—a genre, which by its very nature, can elicit a variety of responses from humor to compassion to laughter? A poem can capture a feeling, present a situation, and make children feel that they're not alone in their efforts to understand themselves and others. The poems in this book aren't overly sentimental or unrealistic. Through humor, whimsy, and down-to-earth language, they acknowledge the real feelings children have and the situations they find themselves in.

The Four Sections of the Book

The collection is divided into four sections to make it easier to use. The first set of poems, "Getting Together," addresses the important topics of making and maintaining friendships; helping each other through encouragement, cooperation, and listening; and respecting each other and all living things.

"The Best Me I Can Be" introduces qualities that a child can strive for—honesty, integrity, generosity, patience, courage, and the end result of self-respect—once he or she knows what those qualities are. Poems encourage children not only to understand their own feelings but also to be compassionate toward other people.

"Manners and Rules" is full of poems about the basics of being polite. The poems cover topics such as the "magic" words, lining up, using an inside voice, interrupting, and lunchtime etiquette. Safety rules appear in this section, too.

"Getting Along" presents situations involving conflict and shows how children can work out conflicts by cooling down, brainstorming solutions, compromising, negotiating, being fair, and standing up for themselves.

A bibliography for children at the back of the book suggests a book to use with each poem. A bibliography for teachers is also included at the back of the book.

How to Use This Collection

You can use the poems as a weekly or daily reminder for children. Poems can be introduced in those "teachable moments" in the classroom as well, such as when a conflict arises between two students. Or if you already have a values curriculum at circle time or another part of the day, you can use the poems to enrich and enliven your teaching.

Each page contains a poem with a particular focus and accompanying activity. The topics in the book are ones that people continue to learn about their whole lives, but the poems and activities have been geared specifically for the primary learner. There is a wide variety of activities for individuals, partners, groups, and the whole class. Here is a sampling of the activities:

- brainstorming a list or web of friendly phrases for making new friends
- acting out "The Tortoise and the Hare" and other Aesop's fables
- creating a Polite Word Wall with a list of courtesy words
- making a paper chain of the names of children who are kind or caring
- completing poetry frames about qualities children like in themselves
- creating a collaborative class book entitled *We Care!*

- participating in listening circles
- painting a mural or participating in another group activity to experience cooperation
- making posters of safety rules
- playing "The Favorites Game" to discover similarities and differences
- drawing "conflict cartoons" to show how to resolve a conflict
- role-playing situations involving conflict using stuffed animals or puppets
- writing thank-you notes
- writing simple journal entries or poetry in "Feeling Journals"
- making a class book about being brave even when one is scared
- observing, drawing, and writing about a living thing in nature to create nature scrolls
- trying new ways of lining up at the door

The benefits of using this book in your classroom are innumerable. The classroom becomes a community of children who understand how to make friends, solve conflicts, get along together, and respect themselves. Of course, "progress, not perfection" is the order of the day—the goals of the book are lifelong goals. But why not start now when children are young?

Our Class Is Like a Fruit Salad

The kids in our classroom
are like a fruit salad,
with different colors
and different tastes.
We each have our families
and houses and meals
and customs and colors
and shapes.

There's Kwaku, Rosita,
and Yoko and Lee.
There's Muhammad, Ashley,
and Carlos and me.
I'm glad that we're not
all exactly alike
'cause look how exciting
a classroom can be!

Respecting Differences/Enjoying Diversity

Make a special bulletin board entitled "Our Class Is Like a Fruit Salad." Cut out a shape that resembles a large salad bowl. Inside the bowl, each child can attach a personal page including his or her photo, name, and "homeland." To create these pages, send home a sheet like the one at the right so parents can help children complete it.

   If there is room for a world map, run a piece of yarn from each child's face to his or her homeland. Children whose families are from several places can choose one place for the display.

(Place photo here.)

My name is _____.
My family comes from
_____.

What Goes Around

I helped Bo,
Bo helped Mo,
Mo helped Mei,
Mei helped Ray,
Ray helped Bea,
and Bea helped me.
"What goes around comes around."
That's how it ought to be.

Being Helpful

Put the poem in a pocket chart, substituting the names of children in your class for the names in the poem. Create new verses by replacing the word *helped* with *smiled at* or *said hi to*.

Talk about the fact that, in general, the way you interact with other people is the way they will interact with you. Write the sentences at the right on chart paper, and invite children to complete them.

Have children talk about why it's important to be helpful and friendly. Ask what the classroom would be like if everyone helped each other and acted in a friendly way.

If I'm friendly, people are _____ to me.

If I smile, people _____ at me.

If I am helpful, people are _____ to me.

My Best Friend and I

Sometimes we're smiley,
Sometimes we're frowny.
Sometimes we're uppy,
Sometimes we're downy.

But mostly we're caring
and mostly we're sharing
and mostly we're laughy
and yappy and happy!

Maintaining Friendships

Point out that having a friend can be a lot of fun, but that friends make the effort to work out conflicts between them. Make a T-chart on a large sheet of paper. Have children talk about things they like to do with friends and then discuss any conflicts they've had. Write their responses on the chart.

Continue the discussion by asking children how they worked out the conflicts. List their solutions.

Things We Do with Friends	Conflicts We've Had with Friends

Friends Like That

Zipping, gliding,
pedaling, sliding,
falling, landing,
splat!

I fell off my bike
and hurt my hand
and off flew
my favorite hat!

Then Annie and Billy
came running to help me.
It's nice to have friends
like that!

Being Caring

Explain that one of the ways children can show they care is by helping
someone in trouble. Discuss the example in the poem and invite children
to describe times they've showed someone they cared. Have each child
complete and illustrate the following frame:

I showed _____ I cared by _____ .
          (name)

The finished pages can be bound into a powerful collaborative book that
highlights the caring side of each child. The book can be titled *We Care!*

Making New Friends

What's your name?
Would you like to play?
Come and join us.
What do you say?

We all need friends
both old and new.
Our newest friend is
Y-O-U!

Being Inclusive

Hearing and reciting friendly, inclusive phrases can be helpful for children. Brainstorm and record other friendly phrases with the class, such as "Hello," "Hi," "What's your name?" "Come and play with us." Children can follow up by drawing a "Friendly Mural." The mural can be as simple as pairs of children's colorful handprints (shaking hands, holding hands, or giving high fives). Each hand can have the word *Hi* written inside it. Or the mural can show pictures of children playing and working together. Along the top of the mural, print the friendly phrases the children brainstormed.

At My New School

At my old school
when new kids came,
I didn't always
say "Hello."
I don't know why
I didn't try
to say those words,
"Hello" and "Hi."

But now that I
am new at school,
I'm suddenly feeling
pretty shy.
I really hope
someone will try
to say the words,
"Hello" or "Hi."

Having Compassion

Explain that having compassion means you can put yourself
in someone else's place and understand how that person
feels. To help children experience compassion for a new kid,
let them role-play this poem using paper bag puppets or
stuffed animals. One child can be the new kid and the other
child can ask the new child to play, to eat lunch together, or
to come over to her or his house.

Sharing, Caring & Getting Along Scholastic Professional Books

Compliments

On birthdays
kids give compliments,
and my birthday is today.
I'm a little bit nervous
to sit in the circle and
hear what they have to say.

"You're a really good friend,"
said lots of kids.
"You're especially nice," said Dee.
"You're really, really strong!"
"You can draw really well"
is what they said about me!

Giving Compliments

On a child's birthday or during a child's special week, let her or him sit inside a circle and receive compliments. Go around the circle in order and have children take turns giving compliments or "put ups" (as opposed to put downs). Encourage children to compliment each other on their qualities and achievements, rather than on what they own or how they look. Remind the child in the center to thank each classmate. When the circle is complete, you can say, "Emily is a very special person!" and lead the class in applause.

Encouragement

There's a basketball hoop
inside our room,
and we practice shooting
one and all.
We each start where we
feel good
and move back slowly
from the wall.

As kids take shots,
we cheer and clap
and give them tips
on what to do.
It's really *amazing*
how well we shoot
with compliments
and encouragement, too.

Giving Encouragement/Using "Put-Ups"

This is a long-term project. Try it in your classroom with a small
basketball hoop and ball, or with a trash can and beanbags. Mark
off 3 feet from the basket, 6 feet, and so on. Everyone starts at
3 feet and moves back when she or he feels comfortable. As a
child takes shots, the rest of the class offers encouragement. It's
truly amazing what children can do when they feel supported.
The activity also teaches them to start where they feel
comfortable and then to stretch themselves step by step.

Sharing, Caring & Getting Along   Scholastic Professional Books

Cooperation

Some things are fun
to do alone.
Some things are fun
in twos.
Some things are best
if you have a group
and here are just a few:
    jumping a rope
    making a band
    putting on a play
    painting a mural
    building a fort
    and sending a bully away!

Cooperating

Have children do something that requires cooperation; for example, they could form a band, paint a mural, or construct a building in the block area. You could involve the whole class by starting a story and letting each child in turn continue it around the circle. You could also sit in a circle and send a hand squeeze around the circle. When the squeeze gets all the way around, compliment everyone for cooperating. Talk about how every single person squeezed, and that's how the squeeze made it all the way around the circle.

The Ant and the Grasshopper*

"Winter's coming,"
said the ants.
"We'd better get
some food to store."
"I'd rather sing,"
said grasshopper.
"Preparing for winter's
such a bore."
But when the chilly
winter came,

the ants were ready
for the cold,
and grasshopper
was cold and thin.
He wasn't feeling
quite so bold.
The ants were nice—
they let him share.
Next wintertime,
he was prepared!

*variation on Aesop's fable

Working Hard and Taking Care of Yourself/ Having Compassion

Discuss the moral of the poem—that it is important to work hard and take care of yourself the way the ants did. Point out that the ants showed compassion for the grasshopper. Let children take turns acting out the poem.

Have the entire class take turns telling parts of the story of the *Three Little Pigs*. How did the third pig take good care of himself? How did he show compassion for the other two pigs? Invite your class to make up a fable of their own about working hard and taking care of yourself. An example might be two squirrels gathering nuts before winter.

I Listen to You, You Listen to Me

Someone talks and
someone listens.
Listening is a two-way street.
When I listen to you
and you listen to me,
then listening is a two-way treat!

Listening

Put the poem on a pocket chart and read it together with the class. Have children find how many times the words *listen* and *listening* are used in this 6-line poem.

Call the children together for a "listening circle." Ask a question and let each child take a turn giving the answer to the child to his or her right. Remind everyone to listen carefully as each answer is given. Questions can be as simple as "What did you have for breakfast?" or "What is your favorite animal?" At the end of the listening circle, ask the class if they can remember what each child said.

Our Bird Project

Samantha's good at talking,
I am good at writing,
Tom is good at drawing—
so we're cooperating!

Tom finished all the pictures.
I've written lots of words.
Samantha's going to give the report
we made about the birds.

Combining Individual Strengths

Take a survey about the task each child would pick if she or
he was doing a bird project—drawing, writing, or talking.
Tally the results and make a graph.

Or let small groups of children pick a task from a hat:
draw, write, or talk. They can trade tasks according to their
strengths, and some of the tasks can be shared. Then each
group can make a poster about a topic you've been
studying and report on it to the class.

Sharing, Caring & Getting Along Scholastic Professional Books

Alike and Different

I asked José for his favorite food
and his was the same as mine.
But as for sports, he's hoops, I'm skates.
We both like a different kind.

I asked Elise for her favorite game
and hers was the same as mine.
But as for pets, she's dogs, I'm cats.
We both like a different kind.

I asked Denise for her favorite song
and hers was the same as mine.
But as for games, she's jacks, I'm tag.
We both like a different kind.

So ask your classmates what they like.
Try playing the "Favorites Game."
Sometimes they'll like things different from you,
and sometimes just the same.

Recognizing Similarities and Differences

Play the "Favorites Game." Draw a line on the floor with the
word *yes* at one end and *no* at the other. Ask a question such
as "Do you like dogs?" and tell everyone to stand on the line
where they belong. (If they "sort of" like dogs, they would be
in the middle.) Continue to ask questions. It's important for
children to discover that they agree with some children on one
topic and disagree with them on another topic.

Nice Surprises

Janet really surprised her dad.
He had a "happy fit"
when Janet took in the groceries
before he mentioned it.

Peter really surprised Ms. Stein.
She was smiling through and through
when he cleaned up all the messy paints
before she asked him to!

Being Helpful

Brainstorm and record a list of nice surprises that could be done for parents, teachers, or other caregivers. Then give each child a sheet of paper in the shape of a gift box with a frame inside to complete.

Each child can write a nice surprise to do for someone at home or at school. Display the gift boxes on a bulletin board entitled "Our Nice Surprises."

My Nice Surprise

I could _____

for _____ .

All the Living Things

Do trees have feelings just like me?
Are frogs ever happy or sad?
Do bugs feel bad when kids say "yuck"?
Does a butterfly feel glad?

Does a spider get upset inside
when her spiderweb is wrecked?
Would all the millions of living things
just like to get our respect?

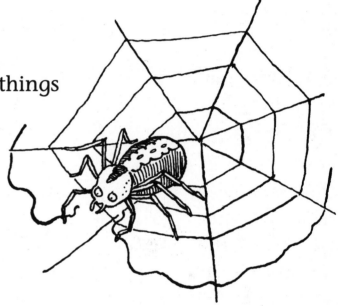

Respecting All Living Things

Give each child a sheet of paper with a brown construction-paper tree trunk pasted on it. Have children sit outside by a tree and draw the rest of the tree along with any living things they see—birds, insects, spiders. Ask them to write about the feelings the tree or one of the other living things might have. Mount their creations on colored paper and attach a string at the top. Hang their nature scrolls on a clothesline in the classroom.

The tree feels like it needs a hug.

The Lion and the Mouse*

A lion caught
a little mouse
who wiggled
and tried to shout,
"Wait, Mr. Lion.
Don't eat me up.
Someday, I promise
to help you out."

Then later, the lion
was caught in a trap
that was made
of sturdy rope.
He roared and roared
his loudest roar
so someone would come,
he hoped.

The mouse came by
and gnawed the rope
and kept the promise
he'd made.
"Thank you, mouse,"
said the jungle king.
"As small as you are,
you came to my aid!"

a retelling of an Aesop's fable

Keeping Promises/ Not Making Quick Judgments

Ask children what they learned from this wise fable. Some of their responses can be turned into time-tested slogans or new slogans. Then each child can pick one to illustrate on mouse-shaped paper. Some possible slogans are shown at the right.

Bind all the pages into a mouse-shaped book entitled *What the Mouse Taught Us*.

- Great things come in small packages.
- Kindness brings kindness in return.
- You reap what you sow.
- What goes around comes around.
- A promise is to keep.
- Don't judge a book by its cover.

Sharing, Caring & Getting Along   Scholastic Professional Books

How People Feel About Me

My aunt says I'm perfect,
My dad says I'm great,
To Grandma and Grandpa,
I'm really first-rate.

They all clearly like me,
I'm sure you'll agree.
But what's most important
is that I like me.

Having Self-Esteem

Make sure children understand what this poem is saying.

Have them finish one of these poetry frames. Note that *I* could be changed to *I'm*.

After children complete their self-esteem frames, let them present their poems to the class.

I like me because
I _____.

I like me because
I _____.

I especially like me
because I _____.

_____ likes me,
_____ likes me,
and I like me because
I _____.

I'm Special, You're Special

You could search on the land
and search in the sea,
and you'd never find someone
exactly like me.

You could search from Hawaii
to Timbuktu,
and you'd never find someone
exactly like you.

You could travel from China
to Tennessee,
and no one would act
exactly like me.

You could check from Egypt
to Kalamazoo,
and no one would think
exactly like you.

For I am me and
you are you.
I am special and
you are, too.

Having Respect for Yourself and Others
Have children decorate a large "campaign" button with their
names in the middle and all the things they like, and qualities
they have, surrounding their names. Then wearing their
campaign buttons, have pairs of children interview each other.
Partners should make sure they know each other's names and
at least one favorite thing or quality. Partners can take turns
introducing each other to the class.

Sharing, Caring & Getting Along Scholastic Professional Books

Making Mistakes

Everybody makes mistakes—
even me and you.
There's just no way around it.
It's something people do.

Have you hurt somebody's feelings
or broken a pen or a vase?
Have you ever forgotten to meet a friend
at a certain time and place?

You can say you're really sorry
or replace the broken pen.
And you can show up right on time
when you meet your friend again.

Taking Responsibility

Create cards for a "Taking Responsibility" game that describe situations in which a choice needs to be made. Some examples are given below.

- You tell a friend you'll play at her house. Then another child asks you to play. Whom do you play with and why?
- You say you'll watch someone's dog, and then you have a family dinner you can't skip. What do you do about the dog?
- You promise you'll clear the table right away, and then a TV show comes on.

Have partners discuss what they would do in each situation and then share their ideas with the class.

Telling the Truth

I *don't* want to tell.
I'd *rather* forget.
Do I *really* have to say?
If I don't tell,
I won't get in trouble
and I can go out and play.

But I'd *better* say.
I *can't* forget.
I think I'll tell *today*.
'Cause telling the truth
feels better than
lying
and hiding
and running away.

Being Honest/Taking Responsibility

There's a lot to talk about in this poem:

- We often have the urge to hide the truth.
- Our conscience nags us to be truthful. (Remember Jiminy Cricket?)
- There may be some consequences for telling the truth, but then you can move on with a clean feeling.

Have children participate in a role-playing game in which one child draws a card that describes a situation such as those shown.

Using puppets, the first child can tell the truth to another child who is acting as a parent, sibling, friend, or teacher. The second child can say, "Thank you for telling the truth."

I broke your toy.

I pushed my sister.

I'm late to school for no good reason.

I didn't do my homework.

Sharing, Caring & Getting Along   Scholastic Professional Books

Someday

Jane stuck up for Tina
when everybody teased.
Jane has the guts to say what she thinks
when no one else agrees.

Someday I hope I have the nerve
to do whatever's right.
I didn't have the guts today.
But tomorrow I just might.

Having Integrity (Doing What Is Right)

The word *integrity* is too sophisticated for primary children; however, they still know what it means to do the right thing— even if it's hard to do. ("The right thing" can be especially hard to do in front of other people.)

Invite children to guess what Jane might have said to the children who were teasing Tina. Record their responses. Then make a list called "Good Things to Say to a Bully" on chart paper. Have children make a border, and post the list in the classroom for future reference.

Patience

I'm growing some patience
inside of me
'cause I need it in different ways:
    to finish a picture
    to wait my turn
    to hear what people say.
I'm growing some patience
inside of me
'cause I use it *every* day.

Having Patience

To explain patience, describe the opposite of patience
(restlessness; being antsy, wiggly, or fidgety; doing things too
quickly; not wanting to wait your turn; not wanting to wait for a
smaller child or someone who's taking a while to do something).

    Reproduce the poem on a pocket chart. Ask children to brain-
storm replacements or variations for lines 4–6. Write their ideas
on pocket chart strips with the authors' initials at the ends of the
strips. Reread the poem with the new lines in place.

Tortoise and Hare Have a Race*

The hare was very
far ahead.
He didn't need to run.
Because he was so
sure he'd win,
he had a little fun.
But tortoise never
stopped to rest
until the race was done.
You won't believe
who came in first.
So can you guess
who won?

*a retelling of an Aesop's fable

Being Persistent (Sticking to It)

Discuss the moral of Aesop's fable—although the tortoise didn't seem to have a chance to win, he never gave up. He just kept going, slowly but surely, and he won the race!

Set up a "race course" in your room and let children act out the poem. You may want to fill in a few details, for example, that the hare relaxed by the roadside and fell asleep during the race. Encourage children to talk about the moral in their own words.

At the School Fair

My good friend Jim
won a bear that's red.
My good friend Jim
won a bear that's blue.
My good friend Jim
gave a bear to me,
and I said, "Thanks!
That's nice of you!"

Being Generous/Saying "Thank you"
Talk about how generosity and sharing are expressed
in the poem. Invite children to list the ways they
share in the classroom or at home.

Start a Polite Word Wall, starting with *Thanks* or
Thank you. Feature one polite word or phrase each
week. Place an arrow next to the featured word.

Sharing, Caring & Getting Along Scholastic Professional Books

Feelings

There's happy, embarrassed,
and silly and sad.
There's excited, delighted,
and frightened and glad.

I've had lots of feelings
already today.
And Mom says it's only been
half of a day!

Identifying Feelings

Copy the poem onto pocket chart strips and have
children talk about the feelings expressed in it. It's
important for them to be able to identify their
feelings so that they understand themselves and
don't take their feelings out on others. Have children
write in "Feelings Journals" about their own feelings
by completing some or all of the phrases shown.

    As children share one of their entries with the class, let
them hold up a paper plate attached to a stick. The paper plate
should have a face with the appropriate feeling drawn on it.

I felt happy when _____.
I felt embarrassed when
_____
I felt angry when _____.
I felt excited when _____.

Sharing, Caring & Getting Along   Scholastic Professional Books

Feeling Sad

I felt sad
when
Taffy died—
Taffy was
my cat.

My father
hugged me
when I
cried,
and I was
glad for
that.

Expressing Sadness

In their "Feelings Journals" have children write about and illustrate a situation that made them sad. They can use the frame, "I felt sad when _____." Older children can make a poem by using the following frame:

I felt sad when _____.
I felt sad when _____.
I felt sad when _____,
but I felt happy when _____.

Call on volunteers to read their sentences or poems to the class.

Sharing, Caring & Getting Along Scholastic Professional Books

Scared and Brave

Scared and brave can go together.
It's strange but yet it's true.
Think of times that you were scared
but did what you needed to do:

doing things you'd never done,
facing someone mean and strong,
telling when you made mistakes,
deciding what was right or wrong.

Think of things you were scared to do
or things you were scared to say.
Then think about how brave you were
to do them anyway.

Having Courage

Compile a class book entitled *Scared and Brave*. Have each child
make a page for the book in which he or she completes the
phrase, "I felt scared when I _____, but I did it anyway!"
This book can serve as an inspiration to children who are feeling
scared about doing something that will take courage.

Listening

I listen mostly with my ears,
but I also listen with my eyes.
I look at your face to see how you feel—
sometimes it's a surprise.

I listen mostly with my ears—
that's a really good place to start.
But I learn a lot about you
when I listen with my heart.

Listening Carefully, with Compassion

Have children "listen" to you as you pantomime four emotions: sad, happy, shy, and angry. Ask them to guess how you're feeling by listening with their eyes.

Tell children to dictate or write memories from when they were younger. Form a listening circle in which they share their memories. Encourage them to listen with their ears, eyes, and hearts. Note that having children write the memories first allows you to help them condense any long stories.

Sharing, Caring & Getting Along Scholastic Professional Books

Morning Greeting

Each morning
when I first arrive,
I say "Hello,"
or I say "Hi."
My teacher greets me
with a smile,
a handshake,
or a big high five!

Greeting People

You may want to practice some form of these greetings with children every morning. You can also put the poem on the pocket chart and let children underline the four words that begin with the letter h—*Hello, Hi, handshake,* and *high five.* Tell pairs of children to practice the greetings with which they are comfortable.

Invite children to brainstorm other greetings to say at the beginning and end of the day. Make a giant greeting card that contains their suggestions inside. Write "Our Greeting Card" on the cover. Display the card on a bulletin board or in a prominent place in the classroom.

The Thank-You Note

Dear Mr. Jeremy Wong,
Thanks for playing those cool songs
and teaching our class about your guitar
and having everyone sing along.

(Jeremy Wong's my father
and I can tell you true.
He really liked the thank-you notes
from me and all of you.)

Expressing Gratitude

Whenever guests come to the classroom, have children write thank-you notes to show their gratitude and to describe what they learned from the presentations.

Let children use puppets or stuffed animals to act out other situations in which a thank you is appropriate. At the end of the activity, thank all of the children for their good work!

Sharing, Caring & Getting Along   Scholastic Professional Books

Please

"Pass the peanut butter, please."
"Could we please go sledding now?"
"Could you please untie my shoe?"
"Please, could we get a horse or cow?"

I didn't get the horse or cow,
but it's polite to say a "please."
It never hurts to try it out.
It sure helps people listen to *me*.

Please, pass the jam!

Saying "Please"

Feature *please* as the polite word of the week. Add it to the Polite Word Wall if you haven't already done so. Let children decorate a poster with the word *please* and post it in the classroom. Whenever anyone uses the word appropriately, put a marble in a jar. When the jar is full, give the class a surprise.

"Excuse Me"

"Excuse me.
Can I please get by?"

"Excuse me.
I've got something to say."

"Excuse me.
I didn't mean to bump."

Excuse me's
a handy thing to say!

Saying "Excuse Me"

Excuse me can be your Polite Word of the Week. Add it to the other courtesy words on the Polite Word Wall. Move the arrow to *Excuse me* so everyone knows which words the class is working on.

Copy the poem onto pocket chart strips. Highlight the verses one at a time and read them together. Ask volunteers to act out the following scenes using stuffed animals:

- Several children are standing in a circle talking, blocking the path of another child who needs to get by.
- Two children are talking. A third child has something important to tell one of them.
- One child bumps another child by mistake.

Notice every time someone in the classroom says "Excuse me."

Magic Words

"Thank you . . ."
"May I . . ."
"Sorry . . ."
"Please . . ."
are magic words—
don't you agree?

They help you
fix your big mistakes
and other silly goofs
you make.

They're perfect
when you ask for things
or thank your friends
for gifts they bring.

"Excuse me . . ."
"Sorry . . ."
"Thank you . . ."
"Please . . ."
They work like magic—
take it from me!

Using "Magic" Courtesy Words
Challenge children to think of situations in which they could use the magic courtesy words *thank you, may I, sorry, please,* and *excuse me.* Add *may I* and *sorry* to the Polite Word Wall.

On a rabbit-shaped sheet of paper, let each child dictate or write a sentence with a magic word in it. Create a "Magic Words" bulletin board on which their "courteous rabbits" are coming out of a magician's top hat.

Interrupting

They say I interrupt a lot
(and I agree it's true)—
my teacher, my mother,
my sister, my brother,
and even my best friend Stu.

I'm trying to let everyone
finish a sentence
and say what they want to say.
I'm trying to listen and wait for my turn
and I'm getting much better each day!

Getting Attention Politely/Not Interrupting

Discuss the poem with children and brainstorm a list of situations in which interruptions frequently occur (a teacher or child is talking in class, two people are trying to solve a conflict, an adult is on the telephone). Encourage children to listen carefully and make a special effort not to interrupt you or other children. Remind someone who interrupts to say "Excuse me" or "Sorry."

Then form a circle and introduce "Interrupting Irvin." Irvin can be a stuffed animal or stick puppet. As you tell a familiar story, have children pass Irvin around the circle. When a child has Irvin, she or he interrupts your story by saying such things as "Hey!" "I need—" "I want—" and "Can I—?" Then put Interrupting Irvin away and tell the story without interruption. Discuss the differences between the two situations.

A Clean Me

I brushed my teeth,
I combed my hair,
I washed my hands
and face with care.

I'm really clean.
I'm not a mess.
I'll stay this way
until recess!

Being Reasonably Clean

It's certainly okay for children to get dirty—this poem is more about reasonable hygiene. Children might be interested to know that being clean and orderly can actually help a person think straight.

Divide a sheet of paper into four sections and write the title "A Clean Me" at the top. Let children draw pictures of four things they can do to start the day clean.

Lining Up

Lining up at school
can be pretty hard to do.
I want to be first and so does Josh,
and maybe you do, too.

If people cut or push,
then they end up in the back.
They end up in the back
of the whole darn pack.

Our teacher has a sticker
for a child in the line.
Sometimes the child is 4th or 10th.
It changes every time.

So now it doesn't matter—
where we line up is just fine,
'cause we each could be a winner
if we're *anywhere* in line.

Lining Up in a Considerate Way

By its nature, lining up can bring out the worst in a
classroom of children. Try giving stickers or recognition
to positions in line other than first by pulling an ordinal
number from a hat after the children are lined up. This
can help take the focus off the first position in line.

Sharing, Caring & Getting Along Scholastic Professional Books

Inside and Outside

By mistake, I bumped into my friend
and shouted in his ear.
The teacher said,
"This classroom's small.
You'd better slow down in here.
But when we go outside again,
then you can run around
and jump and hop and whoop and scream
and make all sorts of sounds."

Using an Inside Voice and Pace

Help children pinpoint what an inside voice sounds like by being the conductor of a classroom chorus. Sit in a circle together and recite a poem or nursery rhyme such as "Mary Had a Little Lamb." First say it so softly that it's hard to hear. Then say it too loudly for the classroom. (Use hand motions to bring the decibels up and down.) Finally recite the poem in a voice that's appropriate for the classroom! Once this inside voice has been established, invite each child to take a turn telling the child on the right what her or his favorite color is, using a full sentence and an inside voice.

Lunchtime Manners

Keeping your mouth closed
whenever you chew
can make it much nicer
to eat lunch with you.

Using your napkin
and wiping off food
gets rid of the goo
when you are all through.

Tossing and recycling
are good things to do.
While you clean up your lunch,
you help the earth, too.

Using Manners When You Eat

Have pairs of children brainstorm lunchtime rules and
manners for a special list entitled "A Bunch of Lunchtime
Manners." Then come together as a class and share ideas.
Write a final list on a large poster shaped like a lunch box.
Post the list where children eat snacks or lunch. Some children may not have been told about mealtime manners,
and this list can make a big difference for them.

Sharing, Caring & Getting Along   Scholastic Professional Books

Rules at School

No pushing on the playground
or running in the hall.
No jumping from the jungle gym
or hogging of the ball.

No wrestling in the classroom
or cutting in the line.
No pinching and no biting
and no hitting, rain or shine.

Whatever we are doing
there seems to be a rule.
I guess that's really the only way
that we stay safe at school.

Following Safety Rules/Being Considerate

There are many school rules listed in this poem. Have children come up with ten important school rules, starting with the word *NO* written in capital letters. Write the rules on pocket chart strips with authors' initials at the ends of the strips. Then let each child copy and illustrate one of the rules for a special bulletin board called "Rules at School."

Manners on the Monkey Bars

Sally goes first
and then comes Fern.
On the monkey bars,
they wait their turn.

Tom goes next
and then comes Lars.
They don't mess around
on the monkey bars.

Fern and Sally,
Tom and Lars,
all mind their manners
on the monkey bars!

Taking Turns

Brainstorm and record situations in the classroom and on the playground when it is important to wait your turn—playing games, doing popular classroom jobs, using class or playground equipment, and so on. Next reproduce the following rhyming couplet and give a copy to each child:

> When I wait my turn with everyone,
>
> then _____ is lots more fun!

Children can fill in indoor or outdoor activities in the blank and sign their names. Compile finished creations in a class collaborative book entitled *Taking Turns*.

Sharing, Caring & Getting Along Scholastic Professional Books

Safe Riding

You need to stop
at stop signs
and to signal with
your hand.

But most important,
your helmet
can protect you
if you land.

Being Safe on a Bike

Give children materials to create posters about bike safety. Some
possible topics are signaling, turning left, riding with traffic, wearing a helmet, stopping at stop signs, and making eye contact
with drivers. Have them present their posters to the class, and
display the finished products around the classroom.

Hold a bike rodeo in which children bring (and share) their
bicycles. They can practice the safety rules on the blacktop.

Part 1: The Problem

> I'm very mad at Johnny Trout. I want to hit and scream and shout. But if I let myself cool down, Then maybe we can work it out.

Solving a Conflict

"Part 1: The Problem" and "Part 2: Working It Out" on the next page show the steps in conflict resolution. Use the poems as a mini-play that can be acted out by two children. You might want to have them use stuffed animals or puppets. For older children who can read the poem, hand out copies of both poems, divide the class into "Johnny" and "the castle builder" and read in unison.

Explain that conflict happens all the time—it's part of life—and that everyone needs tools to deal with it. The tool described here is cooling down before trying to solve a problem. Methods for cooling down include taking deep breaths, counting backward, and taking a walk. Emphasize that cooling down doesn't mean you're giving up your point of view.

Sharing, Caring & Getting Along Scholastic Professional Books

Part 2: Working It Out

You wrecked my nice, big castle
when you just came running by.
I worked so hard to build it—
it used to be this high.

I didn't mean to do it
and you called me nasty names.
But I could build it up again
and make it look the same.

And I could say
I'm sorry
that I called you
all those names!

Solving a Conflict (continued)

Let children discuss the steps in the conflict resolution presented in the poem (cooling down, talking about feelings, finding solutions). They will have to unravel what happened, the way a teacher sometimes does.

Make up "Conflict Cards" describing a problem between two children and place them facedown in a stack. Have partners choose a card and then brainstorm solutions to the conflict. Ask them to share their ideas with the class. Conflicts may include cutting in line, damaging someone's work or property inside or outside the room, refusing to share, tripping someone by mistake, and leaving out someone in a social situation.

Good Sports

Terry used to make kids mad
by boasting when he won.
But now, he always says, "Good game!"
and the games are lots more fun.

Tomeka used to dribble and dribble
and never pass the ball.
But now she lets her teammates play.
She passes to them all.

Robert used to have a fit
whenever he didn't win.
But now he says, "Too bad we lost.
Next week, we'll play again."

Being a Good Sport

Good sportsmanship is appreciated at any age. Start a web entitled "Being a good sport." By brainstorming ideas, everyone in the class will be "on the same page" when situations come up on the playground or when playing inside games. Examples include the following:

- not boasting about a win/being a modest winner
- not being a sore loser/losing with grace
- not hogging the ball/sharing the ball with teammates
- taking turns on the field if there are too many players
- choosing teams in a considerate way
- using a fair method to decide who goes first
- using appropriate physical force
- following the game rules

Display the web on a bulletin board and add to it whenever a new situation arises.

Equal Shares

When we have a snack,
we sit in chairs
and each one gets
an equal share
'cause that's the
only way
it's fair.

If we have twelve
for three of us,
we each get four
and not one more.
We split it up
in equal shares
'cause we agree
it's only
fair.

Being Fair

Act out this poem using a real snack or some small item, such as color cubes, that can be divided equally. Divide the class into groups of three or four and give each group a handful of items to share evenly. If they can't share the items evenly, groups will need to figure out what to do (ask for more, give some back, divide the last item into little pieces). Invite groups to come together and share their strategies with the whole class.

They Both Want the Same Toy

Now they could pull
and they could yell
and they could get
redder and redder.

Or they could take turns
by flipping a coin
or they could
play together!

Brainstorming Solutions to a Conflict

Talk about how solving a conflict involves brainstorming solutions that are agreeable to all parties. Have children describe the problem in this poem and the three solutions or outcomes (fighting, taking turns, sharing).

Then have children draw two frames of a cartoon strip. In the first frame they can show two children or animals fighting over a toy. In the second frame they can draw a solution to the problem. Ask children to place their cartoons on their desks and let everyone walk around the room to admire each other's work. Then glue all the cartoons onto a large sheet of paper with the heading "Conflict Cartoons" as if they were from the comics page of a newspaper.

Nancy's Bad Morning

Nancy couldn't find her sock
and she was late to school.
So she pushed Nate
and teased Sal
and broke a couple of rules.

Jerry asked her what was wrong.
She had a lot to say.
"No wonder you're angry," Jerry said.
"But it's still not okay
to push and tease and mess around
with everyone else's day."

Letting Out Feelings Appropriately/ Listening with Compassion

Ask children if, like Nancy, they've ever come to school angry and felt like being mean to other children. Talk about productive ways to let anger out (hit pillows, talk to a friend, write about it, tell the teacher).

Make a T-chart like the one shown listing some of the things that can happen on a particularly bad day and a good day.

Conclude by explaining that having good days and bad days happens to everyone.

bad day	good day

It's Only Fair

My older brother
stays up till nine,
and Mom and Daddy
say okay.

It's only fair
when I'm his age,
I'll stay up, too—
I just can't wait!

Being Treated Fairly

Ask children if they think it's fair that older siblings get to do
more than younger ones, such as having a later bedtime. Then
create a "wishing tree" using a branch of a tree or a paper tree
mounted on a bulletin board. Give each child a small colored
square on which to write or dictate a privilege or activity he or
she would like to do at an older age. (Many of the privileges
may be things children see their older siblings or friends
getting to do.) Then let children tape or hang their signed
wishes on the wishing tree.

56

Words That Hurt

Sticks and stones
can break my bones,
and words can hurt some, too.
But I don't let them get to me—
I've got things I can do.

If someone's throwing
words around
and trying to ruin my day,
well, I can always walk away
or say, "Don't talk to me that way!"

Taking Care of Yourself/Dealing with Put-Downs

Remind children of the traditional rhyme, "Sticks and stones may break my bones, but words can never hurt me." The saying isn't quite true, but a person can deal with put-downs in a way that makes them less hurtful.

Create a class poster titled "What to Do About Put-Downs." Have children suggest alternatives to dealing with harmful words. Copy each suggestion onto a card, and place the cards in a bag. Pairs of children can draw a card from a bag and act out the situation described. It's important for them see these situations acted out so that they have a model in their minds if a put-down comes their way. After the role-playing, attach the cards to the poster.

A Place That's Fair

Respecting,
Listening,
Being caring.

Cooperating,
Helping,
Sharing.

Our classroom is a place that's fair
'cause all the children really care.

Building a Caring Classroom Community

Add a paper loop to a growing chain every time a child
is kind or caring or fair to someone else in the classroom.
The loop should have the child's name written on it.
Some of the acts of caring could be sharing fairly, listening, helping, and cooperating.

Bibliography for Children

Respecting Differences/ Enjoying Diversity (page 9)

How My Parents Learned to Eat by Ina Friedman (Houghton Mifflin, 1984) This elegantly told story of a mother and father from different cultural backgrounds reinforces the theme of respecting diversity.

Being Helpful (page 10)

Giving by Shirley Hughes (Candlewick Press, 1993) In this charming story, a little girl gives to and receives from lots of different people in her extended family.

Maintaining Friendships (page 11)

Matthew and Tilly by Rebecca C. Jones (Puffin Books, 1995) This book shows the ups and downs of friendship. Like most good friends, Matthew and Tilly play together, have disagreements, and make up.

Being Caring (page 12)

The Rag Coat by Lauren Mills (Little, Brown, 1991) In this sensitively written book, the women in a community show they care by making a rag coat for Minna, a little girl in need. The children at school apologize for teasing Minna and come to care for her, too.

Being Inclusive (page 13)

Will I Have a Friend? by Miriam Cohen (Macmillan, 1967) This story fits in well with the theme, as it describes Jim's successful efforts to find a friend on the first day of school.

Having Compassion (page 14)

Angel Child, Dragon Child by Michele Maria Surat (Scholastic, 1989) A lonely Vietnamese girl in an American school must deal with insensitivity, but ultimately receives a special gift from a new friend.

Giving Compliments (page 15)

Rosie and Michael by Judith Viorst (Atheneum, 1974) Viorst provides charming examples of giving compliments as best friends Rosie and Michael describe what they like about each other—warts and all.

Giving Encouragement/Using "Put-Ups" (page 16)

Crow Boy by Tara Yashima (Viking, 1955) When a new teacher appreciates Crow Boy's talents, he gains self-esteem.

Cooperating (page 17)

Swimmy by Leo Lionni (Random House, 1963) Cooperation is the key in this book about a school of little fish that swim together in the shape of a large fish to scare off any predators.

Working Hard and Taking Care of Yourself/Having Compassion (page 18)

Aesop's Fables illustrated by Charles Santore (Random House, 1999) Embellish this fable by reading other versions and showing the beautiful illustrations. Note that in the original story, the ants show no compassion for the grasshopper.

Listening (page 19)

Sing Sophie! by Dale Ann Dodds (Candlewick Press, 1997) Nobody listens to Sophie's singing until a storm frightens the baby and her singing calms him down.

Combining Individual Strengths (page 20)

Frederick by Leo Lionni (Random House, 1967) As the mice prepare for winter, they don't realize that Frederick's strength is poetry writing. His poems raise their spirits in the depths of winter when the food is nearly gone.

Recognizing Similarities and Differences (page 21)

Stellaluna by Jannell Cannon (Harcourt, 1993) Stellaluna the bat and her bird friends marvel at how different they are and yet how alike they feel.

Being Helpful (page 22)

A Chair for My Mother by Vera B. Williams (Greenwillow, 1982) A little girl saves enough pennies to buy a chair for the hard-working mother.

Respecting All Living Things (page 23)

The Snail's Spell by Joanne Ryder (Viking, 1992) This beautifully told narrative helps readers imagine what it feels like to be a snail. The book will give children ideas for their nature scrolls.

Keeping Promises/ Not Making Quick Judgments (page 24)

Aesop's Fables illustrated by Charles Santore (Random House, 1999) This tale of the lion and the mouse, which is briefly told and beautifully illustrated, can be used to embellish the poem and reinforce the themes.

Having Self-Esteem (page 25)

Amazing Grace by Mary Hoffman (Dial Books, 1991) In this story of determination and self-esteem, Grace believes in herself and makes her dreams come true.

Having Respect for Yourself and Others (page 26)

Fish Is Fish by Leo Lionni (Pantheon, 1970) Fish gets into trouble when he tries to imitate his adventurous friend, the frog. Fish comes to accept himself just the way he is and to see that his small pond is beautiful.

Taking Responsibility (page 27)

Spinky Sulks by William Steig (Farrar, Straus and Giroux, 1988) Spinky sulks when his family hurts his feelings. The book's resolution introduces another aspect of making mistakes—forgiveness.

Being Honest/Taking Responsibility (page 28)

The Honest-to-Goodness Truth by Patricia C. McKissack (Atheneum, 2000) Libby tells everyone her truthful thoughts with no regard to anyone's feelings.

Having Integrity (Doing What Is Right) (page 29)

Bailey the Big Bully by Lizi Boyd (Viking, 1989)* This book gives children a good model of how to stand up to a bully.

Having Patience (page 30)

Lizard's Song by George Shannon (Greenwillow Books, 1992) A lizard shows great patience as he tries to teach a bear how to sing.

Being Persistent (Sticking to It) (page 31)

Aesop's Fables illustrated by Charles Santore (Random House, 1999) Reading children another version of the story of the tortoise and the hare will reinforce the theme of persistence.

* indicates out-of-print book

Being Generous/
Saying "Thank you" (page 32)

I Know a Lady by Charlotte Zolotow
(Greenwillow Books, 1986) Sally describes an
old lady's generosity and friendliness toward the
children in the neighborhood.

Identifying Feelings (page 33)

Lilly's Purple Plastic Purse by Kevin Henkes
(Greenwillow Books, 1996) This story adds
substance to the poem as Lilly goes through a
kaleidoscope of feelings.

Expressing Sadness (page 34)

The Tenth Good Thing about Barney by Judith
Viorst (Atheneum, 1971) A grieving boy thinks
of ten good things about his cat that has died.

Having Courage (page 35)

There's Something in My Attic by Mercer Mayer
(Dial Books, 1988) The feeling of being both
"scared and brave" is well illustrated in this book
in which a young girl goes up to the attic to
lasso her nightmare.

Listening Carefully,
with Compassion (page 36)

Grandpa's Face by Eloise Greenfield (Philomel
Books, 1988) Tamika "listens" with her eyes in
this story. At first she's frightened by her grandfather's mean faces as he rehearses for a play.
Then Tamika realizes that Grandfather will never
use mean faces, or feelings, toward her.

Greeting People (page 37)

Hello, Gnu, How Do You Do? by Barbara Shook
Hazen (Doubleday, 1990)* This book presents
manners in the context of situations involving
endearing animal characters.

Expressing Gratitude (page 38)

Manners by Aliki (Greenwillow Books, 1990)
Good manners are the topic of Aliki's charming
book that touches on many aspects of being
polite and considerate.

Saying "Please" (page 39)

It's a Spoon, Not a Shovel by Caralyn Buehner
(Dial Books, 1995) Children are given very
humorous situations and multiple-choice
questions to find out if their manners are
monstrous or marvelous.

Saying "Excuse Me" (page 40)

Perfect Pigs by Marc Brown and Stephen
Krensky (Little, Brown, 1983) The pigs in this
story offer a perfect way to teach manners pain-
lessly.

Using "Magic" Courtesy Words (page 41)

Mary Louise Loses Her Manners by Diana Cuneo
(Doubleday, 1999) When Mary Louise hears
herself saying "flies" and "spank you," instead of
"please" and "thank you," she realizes she's lost
her manners and needs to find them again.

* indicates out-of-print book

Getting Attention Politely/ Not Interrupting (page 42)

Oops! Excuse Me Please! and Other Mannerly Tales by Bob McGrath (Barrons, 1998) This book provides humorous situations and illustrations related to good manners.

Being Reasonably Clean (page 43)

Pigsty by Mark Teague (Scholastic, 1994) Wendell's room becomes so messy that a herd of pigs moves in.

Lining Up in a Considerate Way (page 44)

Mrs. Peloski's Substitute by Joanne Oppenheim (Dodd, Mead, 1987)* Classroom manners go out the window when a substitute comes to Mrs. Peloski's classroom.

Using an Inside Voice and Pace (page 45)

No, David! by David Shannon (Scholastic, 1998) David definitely doesn't know about inside voices and behavior in this outrageous look at a boy who is rambunctious but still very much loved.

Using Manners When You Eat (page 46)

Mouse Mess by Linnea Riley (Scholastic, 1997) A hungry mouse makes quite a mess as it hunts for a snack in the kitchen.

Following Safety Rules/ Being Considerate (page 47)

Officer Buckle and Gloria by Peggy Rathman (G. P. Putnam's Sons, 1995) The elementary school children start paying attention to Officer Buckle's safety rule speeches when he brings along Gloria, the police dog.

Taking Turns (page 48)

Dinosaurs Beware by Marc Brown (Little, Brown, 1984) Appealing dinosaurs illustrate safety tips.

Being Safe on a Bike (page 49)

Bike Trip by Betsy Maestro (HarperCollins, 1992) A boy recounts a pleasant family bike trip, including safety rules.

Solving a Conflict (page 50)

The Honey Hunters by Francesca Martin (Candlewick Press, 1992) In this African folktale, the animals have a hard time sharing the honey, and children will see what happens when conflicts aren't worked out.

Solving a Conflict (continued) (page 51)

The Owl and the Woodpecker by Brian Wildsmith (Oxford University Press, 2000) When the owl and the woodpecker become neighbors, there's lots of conflict. But a storm that blows in changes woodpecker's perspective.

Being a Good Sport (page 52)

Old Turtle's Soccer Team by Leonard Kessler (Greenwillow Books, 1988)* Old Turtle not only teaches the other animals how to play soccer but also the meaning of good sportsmanship.

Being Fair (page 53)

The Doorbell Rang by Pat Hutchins (Greenwillow Books, 1986) Every time the doorbell rings, there are more children to share Ma's cookies.

Brainstorming Solutions to a Conflict (page 54)

The Biggest Pumpkin Ever by Steven Kroll (Holiday House, 1984) Two mice are growing the same pumpkin, but they aren't aware of each other. Their solution to ownership is a great lesson in compromise and sharing.

* indicates out-of-print book

**Letting out Feelings Appropriately/
Listening with Compassion (page 55)**
*Alexander and the Terrible, Horrible, No Good,
Very Bad Day* by Judith Viorst (Atheneum,
1972) Everything goes wrong, and Alexander
learns that "some days are just like that."

Being Treated Fairly (page 56)
The Pain and the Great One by Judy Blume
(Bradbury Press, 1984) Two siblings perceive
each other as troublemakers and think their parents love the other one better.

**Taking Care of Yourself/
Dealing with Put-Downs (page 57)**
The Quarreling Book by Charlotte Zolotow
(Harper, 1963) This book shows how your
words and actions (both quarrelsome and kind)
affect those around you.

**Building a Caring Classroom
Community (page 58)**
It's Mine! by Leo Lionni (Knopf, 1986) Three
frogs that live together think only of themselves
but end up as a sharing, caring community.

Bibliography for Teachers

Dodge, Ellen Pritchard. *Communication Lab.*
E. Moline, IL: LinguiSystems, 1998.

Kreidler, William J. *Teaching Conflict Resolution
Through Children's Literature.* New York:
Scholastic Professional Books, 1995.

Popov, Linda Kavelin. *The Family Virtues Guide.*
New York: Plume, 1997.

*Prutzman, Priscilla, Lee Stern; M. Leonard
Burger, and Gretchen Bodenhamer. *The
Friendly Classroom for a Small Planet.*
Philadelphia: New Society Publishers, 1988.

*Rich, Dorothy. *MegaSkills: How Families Can
Help Children Succeed in School and Beyond.*
Boston: Houghton Mifflin, 1998.

* indicates out-of-print book

Notes